ALBANIA POLITICAL IMPRISONMENT AND THE LAW

Amnesty International Publications

First published 1984 by Amnesty International Publications
1 Easton Street, London WC1X 8DJ, United Kingdom

© Copyright Amnesty International Publications 1984

ISBN 0 86210 078 X
AI Index: EUR 11/04/84
Original Language: English

Printed by Shadowdean Limited, Mitcham, Surrey

Contents

***A plan of Spac labour camp 303 based on prisoners' sketches
appears on pages 39 and 40.**

The People's Socialist Republic of Albania

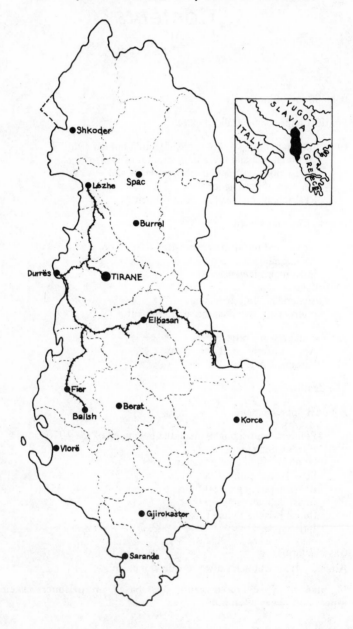

Political imprisonment and the law

Amnesty International's concerns in Albania include:

- the imprisonment of prisoners of conscience;
- legislation which severely restricts the exercise of internationally recognized human rights;
- breaches of internationally recognized standards of fair trial;
- allegations of the torture and ill-treatment of detainees, in particular during investigation proceedings;
- the use of the death penalty.

This report presents information on the laws under which political prisoners are charged, tried and detained; it also describes their implementation in cases known to Amnesty International.

Penal legislation in Albania is explicitly ideological and is officially characterized as a "weapon" in the class struggle. Furthermore, provisions defining political offences are loosely formulated and this facilitates their broad interpretation by courts. The report examines certain aspects of the judicial process which breach international standards, in particular those involving the denial of the accused's right to defence counsel during investigation proceedings and trial. Amnesty International is concerned, moreover, because former political prisoners have often alleged that they were beaten or otherwise ill-treated during investigation proceedings in order to force them to make "confessions".

The report describes conditions in the forced labour camp of Spac which do not conform to the international standards set down in the United Nations Standard Minimum Rules for the Treatment of Prisoners. The available information about conditions in other centres where political prisoners are detained indicates that these, too, fail to conform to international standards.

The report is based on official and unofficial sources. The official sources include published documents such as the Constitution of 1976, the Criminal Code of 1977 and the Code of Criminal Procedure of 1980, as well as other relevant legislation published in Albanian official state gazettes. The unofficial sources have consisted of accounts by former political prisoners who, on release, fled the country, or by their friends and relatives living outside the country. Informants have in many cases requested anonymity for fear of reprisals against their families remaining in Albania. For this reason the report on a number of occasions omits names and other details.

The information in this report concerns primarily the period from the early 1970s to the beginning of the 1980s. However, where current laws or judicial practices were introduced before the 1970s, reference has been made to earlier periods. In addition, the very long sentences prescribed for political offences have meant that it has been necessary to refer to some cases of political prisoners who were sentenced in the 1960s but only released in the 1970s or 1980s.

This report cannot claim to provide a comprehensive picture of political imprisonment as practised today in Albania. This is primarily due to official censorship and to restrictions on freedom of movement. Official sources provide almost no information, apart from legal texts, on the issue of political imprisonment. Albanian citizens cannot travel freely abroad, and only very few succeed in leaving the country illegally.

Although the accounts of refugees undoubtedly sometimes contain inaccuracies and may be suspected of bias, much of the information provided has been internally consistent. In addition, it has been possible to check against each other accounts which were provided independently, by informants who came from different backgrounds and different parts of the country. Lastly, the official legislative framework has provided a basis for verifying the accuracy of information.

Amnesty International considers that the information it has gained concerning human rights violations in Albania, though incomplete, is sufficiently detailed and accurate to merit publication. It has sought the comments of the authorities of the People's Socialist Republic of Albania on the concerns it has raised in this report.

Constitutional and legal provisions affecting human rights

In 1955 Albania ratified the Convention on the Prevention and Punishment of the Crime of Genocide (1948) and the Convention on the Political Rights of Women (1952). It has not, however, ratified the two major United Nations treaties on human rights, the International Covenant on Civil and Political Rights and the International Covenant on Social, Economic and Cultural Rights.

It is the only European country which is not a signatory of the Final Act of the Conference on Security and Cooperation in Europe (Helsinki 1975), commonly known as the "Helsinki Accords".

The present Constitution of the People's Socialist Republic of Albania, promulgated on 28 December 1976, replaced the Constitution of 1946 which had been amended several times during the 1950s and 1960s. Whereas the previous constitution was modelled on those of the Soviet Union and other East European countries, official commentaries on the present one condemn the constitutional developments that have taken place in these countries, which are termed "revisionist" and even "counter-revolutionary". The current Albanian Constitution, on the other hand, is said to embody the "principles formulated by Marx, Engels, Lenin and Stalin, especially in the field of the theory of the dictatorship of the proletariat" (the communist party daily newspaper *Zeri i Popullit* [The Voice of the People] 9 January 1980)—principles from which revisionists are said to have deviated. The Constitution is thus conceived of as an instrument of class struggle. Although it guarantees a number of fundamental human rights, with important specific restrictions on the rights to freedom of conscience, expression and association, it also lays down a general principle limiting the exercise of fundamental rights in cases where the individual and the general interest conflict.

Among the rights guaranteed are:

— Equality before the law, regardless of sex, race, nationality,

social position or material situation (Article 40).
— "Freedom of scientific work and literary and artistic creativity" (Article 51).
— "Freedom of speech, press, organization, association, assembly and public demonstration" (Article 53).
— The right to "unite in various organizations operating in the political, economic, cultural and any other area of the country's life" (Article 54).
— "Inviolability of the person" (Article 56).
— Inviolability of the home (Article 57).
— "Secrecy of correspondence and other means of communication" (Article 58).
— The right to "present petitions, complaints, remarks and suggestions to the competent [state] organs on personal, social and state affairs" (Article 59).

The following articles, however, impose broad restrictions on many of these rights:
— Article 39: "The rights and duties of citizens are established on the basis of the reconciliation of the interests of the individual and those of socialist society, with priority given to the general interest. The rights of citizens are inseparable from the fulfilment of their duties and cannot be exercised in opposition to the socialist order."
— Article 37: "The state recognizes no religion and supports and carries out atheist propaganda in order to implant a scientific materialist world outlook in people."
— Article 55: "The creation of organizations of a fascist, anti-democratic, religious, or anti-socialist nature is prohibited. Fascist, anti-democratic, religious, warmongering and anti-socialist activities and propaganda are prohibited as is the incitement of national and racial hatred."

Amnesty International considers that the provisions of these three articles, in so far as they apply to religious and to non-violent political activity, go far beyond the restrictions on the exercise of human rights which may be imposed in accordance with international human rights standards.

Criminal law and the administration of justice

Criminal law: The current Criminal Code was introduced on 1 October 1977, replacing the previous code of 1952. Article 1 states the aims of the present code and emphasizes that they are primarily political and ideological:

"The penal legislation of the People's Socialist Republic of
Albania expresses the will of the working class and other
working masses and is a powerful weapon of the dictatorship
of the proletariat in the class struggle.

"Penal legislation has the task of defending the socialist
state, the Albanian Party of Labour as the sole political
guiding force of the state and society, socialist property, the
rights and interests of citizens and the whole socialist order
from socially dangerous acts by means of the application of
penal measures against those who commit them.

"An important duty of the penal legislation of the People's
Socialist Republic of Albania is the fight against bureaucracy
and liberalism as the chief dangers to the state of the
dictatorship of the proletariat."

The concept of impartial justice is expressly rejected in various
official comments on the code, which criticize "capitalist" and
"revisionist" states for disguising, in the name of "equal rights for
all" the class character of their penal legislation. Albanian
legislation on the contrary, it is claimed, "does not conceal . . .
[but] greatly stresses . . . that the interests of the Party, as the tip
of the sword of the working class, as faithful spokesman of the will
of the working masses, are predominant in its entire composition"
(*Drejtesia Popullore* [People's Justice] No. 1, 1979, a journal
published by the Supreme Court).

The first section of the Special Part of the Criminal Code of
1977 deals with political crimes, referred to as crimes against the
state. It retains, with few alterations, the provisions of the
corresponding section of the Criminal Code of 1952. As before,
all offences against the state are punishable by non-mandatory
death sentences, with the exception now of the offence of
"incitement to hatred and racial or national discord", for which
the penalty is three to 10 years' imprisonment. However,
confiscation of the accused's property, a penalty previously
applicable to all offences against the state, no longer applies.

Most articles defining offences against the state are loosely
formulated and lend themselves to broad interpretation by the
courts. For example, Article 53, dealing with "sabotage", states:

"An action or lack of action intended to weaken or
undermine state activity or that of the Albanian Party of
Labour, the socialist economy, the organization and
direction of the state and society will be punished by
deprivation of liberty for not less than 10 years or by death."

A comment on Article 53 published in *Drejtesia Popullore* in 1981 appeared to indicate that its interpretation had caused problems but the comment itself offered only very broad guidelines and dubious standards of proof. It cited as an example of "sabotage of state activity" the "issuing of various sublaws . . . not according to and . . . [not furthering] the implementation of state laws, but with counter-revolutionary intent, in violation of these laws or in opposition to them". "Sabotage of the activity of the Albanian Party of Labour" was described as activity opposed to the policy and ideology of the Party "in order to spread bourgeois-revisionist views about the class-struggle, about the dictatorship of the proletariat, about the alliance between the working class and the cooperativist peasantry, etc.". "Sabotage of the organization and direction of the state and society" was characterized as "action or lack of action which is intended to create organizational links which undermine the principle of democratic centralism and open the road to revisionist self-management, [and] which is intended to hinder the regular and normal activity of social organizations through failure to fulfil their tasks or their poor fulfilment."

The article stressed that the existence of "counter-revolutionary intent" was a crucial element of the offence of sabotage but admitted that cases in which this was easy to establish were rare. It recommended two criteria to be applied in assessing cases "in which the offender acts and leaves no traces of sabotage, in which his action or inaction appears rather to be a misuse of function, an appropriation of or damage to socialist property, a simple violation of the equality of citizens or of the rights of workers etc."—in these cases the criteria should be firstly, the gravity of the consequences of the action (or inaction) and secondly, the "personality " of the offender: "what is his attitude towards the people's authority, towards revolution and socialism; what is his history and present attitude, his social circle, his behaviour at work and in society?"

That a very wide range of activities was open to prosecution as sabotage and that considerable numbers of people had been convicted of this offence was indicated in one of the article's conclusions:

"Thus, all the hostile groups which were uncovered—especially during recent years in the military field, in the field of state administration and economic management, in the field of arts and culture and so forth—tried to accomplish their hostile objectives entirely through sabotage in the various spheres of our political, ideological, military, economic and administrative life."

The administration of justice: This is highly centralized. Three of the four chief bodies responsible for this function (the Supreme Court, the Procuracy and the Office of the Investigator General) are appointed by and directly accountable to the People's Assembly—in effect, to the Presidium of the People's Assembly.

The Supreme Court is now responsible for supervising the work of the courts. Formerly this was the task of a Ministry of Justice. The latter was established in 1952 but was abolished in 1966, when the Premier, General Mehmet Shehu, was reported to have stated that "now that the question of socialist legality has become the affair of the nation as a whole, there are no longer any objective reasons justifying its existence".

The organization of the courts is laid down in the Law on Judicial Organization of 1968. In addition to the Supreme Court, there are People's Courts at village, town, town ward and district levels. At the district and Supreme Court levels there are military sections in addition to civil and criminal sections. Benches are composed of both professional and lay judges. The Supreme Court is elected for a four-year term by the People's Assembly; courts at lower levels are elected locally.

The Law on the Procuracy of 1981 states that the Procuracy monitors the implementation of laws by government institutions, courts, investigating bodies, enterprises and citizens, and its tasks include the detection of violations of the law. Procurators are required to monitor the legality of court decisions, to approve decisions for arrest and house searches and to monitor the implementation of laws in prisons and other places of detention.

Albanian procurators are not, however, as in most other Eastern European countries, necessarily involved in the investigation and prosecution of all crimes. They are entitled to be present when investigations are being carried out and to take part in criminal and civil trials, but they are not obliged to do so.

The Procurator General and his deputies are appointed by the People's Assembly; district procurators are appointed by the Presidium of the Assembly and procurators at lower levels by the Procurator General.

Crimes are investigated by officials of the Office of Investigation. Until 1983 this office was part of the Ministry of the Interior but in June that year the People's Assembly passed a bill creating an independent Investigator General's Office. Speakers introducing the bill stated that this new office had been conceived as an "organ of the people's justice". In its work it was to be independent of organs of state administration and of judicial bodies. It would "promote the popular character and revolutionary spirit of our investigating organs, increase objectivity in investigating crimes and strengthen socialist legality". The head of this office is appointed by and responsible to the People's Assembly.

Law enforcement is carried out by the People's Police, responsible for normal policing functions and assisted by an auxiliary force of citizens, and by the large state security service known as the *Sigurimi* (Security); both are bodies of the Ministry of the Interior.

Restrictions on freedom of expression and freedom of conscience

The restrictions on the exercise of these freedoms set out in the Constitution are reinforced by the provisions of Article 55 of the Criminal Code, dealing with "anti-state agitation and propaganda". This article states:

"Fascist, anti-democratic, religious, warmongering or anti-socialist propaganda, as well as the preparation, distribution or the possession for distribution of literature with such a content in order to weaken or undermine the state of the dictatorship of the proletariat are punished by deprivation of liberty for from three to 10 years.

"These same acts, when committed in wartime or when they have caused especially serious consequences are punished by deprivation of liberty for not less than 10 years or by death."

Freedom of expression

The information available to Amnesty International indicates that many political prisoners have been convicted on charges brought under the above article or under the corresponding article of the former Criminal Code, Article 73.

The narrow limits within which the exercise of freedom of expression is permitted are indicated in an article published in *Drejtesia Popullore* in 1977 which stated: "In our country there is no freedom of thought for enemy elements, who, speculating on democracy, try to spread their anti-socialist, reactionary, liberal and decadent bourgeois or revisionist views and ideas in order to introduce disruption and degeneration into all spheres of life, art, culture, the economy and the army."

In practice, it appears that people who express views critical of economic or political conditions in the country are liable to be prosecuted, even if their criticisms are voiced in private conversations. A number of former political prisoners have told Amnesty International that they were convicted on the basis of the testimony of informers or plainclothes *Sigurimi* officials, who in some cases had deliberately provoked them to criticize the authorities.

One former prisoner said he was jailed for three years and interned for another three because of conversations with acquaintances in which he had spoken of the 1973 and 1978 revolts in Spac labour camp (see page 41). He alleged that two *Sigurimi* agents present during the conversations had reported him to the authorities.

Another former prisoner described how he had been pressed by local police officials to inform on his own brother. They began to harass him when he refused and he eventually protested publicly about this at a meeting in his village. As a result he was forced to leave the village, he said. He was subsequently arrested and served a seven-year prison sentence, from 1970 to 1977, after he had been charged with "anti-state agitation and propaganda".

Kostas Moukas, an ethnic Greek, said he was arrested in 1981, during his military service, after he had expressed disagreement with criticisms of the Greek Government made by an officer in the course of a political lecture. In April 1982 he was sentenced in Gjirokaster to eight years' imprisonment. He was released under the amnesty of November 1982 and later fled to Greece.

In another case reported to Amnesty International, a conscript from the north of the country was sentenced in Shkoder in 1981 to eight years' imprisonment after he had been charged with having spoken favourably to fellow-conscripts about King Zog, Albania's pre-war ruler.

Amnesty International has learned also of cases in which charges of having engaged in "anti-state agitation and propaganda" have included accusations that defendants had listened to foreign radio stations. Albanians who watch or listen to Italian, Greek or Yugoslav radio and television broadcasts, which can be received in different parts of the country, tend to be regarded with suspicion by the authorities.

—A former prisoner sentenced to nine years' imprisonment in 1980 (but now outside the country) has stated that the charges against him included allegations that he had watched a Yugoslav television program containing anti-Albanian propaganda—the program was a televised football match, he said.

—In June 1983 an Albanian refugee who had fled to Yugoslavia reported, according to the official Yugoslav newsagency *Tanjug*, that a fellow-villager had been sentenced to 10 years' imprisonment for having listened to *Radio Pristina*, the Albanian-language radio station of the capital of Kosovo province in Yugoslavia.

Official confirmation that listening to foreign radio stations may constitute an indictable offence is to be found in an account published in *Studime Historike*, No. 4, 1981—a quarterly journal published by Tirane university—on the case of the priest Shtjefen Kurti (see below), from which it is clear that the charges of "anti-state agitation and propaganda" brought against him included the accusation that he had listened to "news broadcasts from foreign radio stations and had commented on them".

In recent years Albanians have also reportedly been convicted of "anti-state agitation and propaganda" as a result of their contacts with foreign tourists, or for possessing books or works of art officially disapproved of. Amnesty International has been informed, too, that a prisoner of conscience was serving a second sentence at the beginning of the 1980s because of poems he had written about his previous experiences as a political prisoner.

Freedom of conscience and religion

In 1967 Albania was officially proclaimed "the first atheist state in the world". By the end of that year all forms of organized religious life had been banned, thus concluding the process of suppression of religion that had begun at the close of the Second World War.

According to a religious census taken in 1945, 72.8 per cent of the population was Muslim, 17.1 per cent belonged to the (Christian) Autocephalous Orthodox Church of Albania and 10.1 per cent to the Roman Catholic Church.

In the immediate post-war years the religious communities were deprived of much of their property under the land reform of 1945, education was secularized and religious publications, sermons and other public communications were subjected to state censorship. The appointment of religious functionaries was also controlled by the state. A large number of the religious communities' leaders were interned, imprisoned or executed, often on charges of having collaborated with Fascist forces. After a series of show trials the Roman Catholic Jesuit order was banned in 1946, and the Franciscans in 1947.

State education inculcated atheist doctrine and a strong nationalism in the younger generation; religious belief was officially attacked as having impeded progress and national unity.

Decree No. 743 of 1949, "Concerning Religious Communities" was followed in 1950 and 1951 by decrees which put them under state control and in particular obliged the Roman Catholic Church to break off all relations with the Vatican.

Albania's "Cultural and Ideological Revolution", begun in 1966, intensified the campaign against religion:

—In a speech on 6 February 1967, Enver Hoxha encouraged a movement by young people across the country to close down mosques and churches. Some of these buildings were destroyed, others converted into warehouses or cultural centres.

—A decree in April 1967 turned over all the fixed assets of religious communities to the executive committees of the people's councils in the districts concerned or to agricultural cooperatives, without compensation.

—In September that year it was officially announced that all religious buildings, including 2,169 churches, mosques, monasteries and other religious institutions had been shut down.

—On 13 November Decree No. 4337 annulled the decrees of 1949, 1950 and 1951 on religious communities; the latter were thus deprived of legal status and their functionaries prohibited from exercising their offices.

Decree No. 4337 contravened Article 18 of the 1946 Constitution, then in force, which not only guaranteed freedom of conscience and of faith but also stated: "All religious communities are free in matters concerned with their faith as well as in its practice and outward expression."

According to official accounts, some clergy voluntarily renounced further religious activity, but others resisted and protested "by presenting petitions to the government or to the Presidium of the People's Assembly which distorted the truth and attributed to local government the actions of the youth, or the will expressed by the people to liquidate churches and mosques" (*Studime Historike*, No. 4, 1981).

The anti-religious campaign of 1967 thus saw a further wave of persecution against the clergy. For example, according to one report received by Amnesty International, a group of Orthodox priests from Sarande district were brought to the town of Delvine where they were publicly defrocked and had their beards shaved before a jeering crowd. One member of the group, who resisted this treatment, was reported to have been sentenced to eight years' imprisonment for "anti-state agitation and propaganda".

Others arrested and imprisoned in 1967 and afterwards included the Franciscans Gega Lumaj, Mark Hasi and Zef Plumbi. In the mid-1970s Albanian emigre sources stated that three Roman Catholic titular bishops had been interned or imprisoned after they had conducted religious ceremonies in private. Two of them—Bishops Coba and Fishta—are said to have since died in detention. The third, Bishop Nikoll Troshani, was in Ballsh labour camp in the late 1970s, according to a former prisoner of conscience.

Other clergy who, according to various sources, were reportedly interned or imprisoned during the 1970s included the priests Pjeter Meshkalla, Ndrec Gega, Ndoc Sahatcia, Zef Nikolla, Fran Ilia, Federik Mazi, Injac Gjora, Rrok Gjuraj, Gjergj Vata, Simon Jubani (and his brother Lazer) and the Muslim cleric Sabri Koci. In most cases they were reportedly convicted of "anti-state agitation and propaganda", but Amnesty International does not have details of the charges.

Amnesty International has sought further information on these prisoners and others who were said to be serving sentences in the early 1980s. Among the latter was the priest Fran Mark Gjoni who was allegedly sentenced to 12 years' imprisonment in 1977 for possessing Bibles. Amnesty International was also concerned about the Jesuit Father Ndoc Luli, from Mali Jushit, near Shkoder, who was reported to have been imprisoned in 1980 after he had baptized the children of a relative. Emigre religious sources claimed that he was killed shortly after his imprisonment, but a former political prisoner has stated that Father Luli was in Ballsh labour camp in late 1982.

The fate of many clerics, Muslim and Christian, remains unknown and reports are often conflicting. Amnesty International knows of only one case in which the Albanian authorities have volunteered information and even then the official information has not only contradicted that supplied by unofficial sources but has not been wholly consistent. Amnesty International has not been able to obtain independent confirmation of either version.

The case concerns the Roman Catholic priest Father Shtjefen Kurti. According to both unofficial and official sources, he was first tried and sentenced to 20 years' imprisonment in 1945 after conviction on charges of espionage on behalf of the USA and Great Britain. He was released in 1962 before the expiry of his sentence. His sister gave the following account of what happened subsequently: After his release he went to the village of Gurrez (Kruje district) for a short time before being sent to do parish work in Durres. When churches were closed there in February 1967 he found employment as a warehouse worker in a cooperative. Shortly afterwards he was arrested in Lezhe for having opposed the destruction of a church there by anti-religious militants. He was apparently sentenced to internment in a corrective labour camp. Here he baptized a child secretly at the request of its mother. For this he was tried by a court in Milot in December 1971 and sentenced to death. He was executed in February 1972.

The above account was first published in the foreign press in March 1973. On 28 April 1973 *Radio Tirane* denied that Father Kurti had been executed for baptizing a child and said that he had been executed in 1970 for espionage, economic sabotage and anti-state propaganda.

The case was later referred to in *Studime Historike*, no. 4, 1981, in an article entitled "The Revolutionary Movement against Religion in the Sixties". This stated that Father Kurti's "hostile activity" had come to light in 1967; it had consisted of sabotage, that is, of encouraging and organizing "massive theft" from the agricultural cooperative of Fushe-Milot. He had also engaged in "anti-state agitation and propaganda" it was alleged; this charge was based on meetings he had had with other disaffected persons in which he had allegedly claimed that the political situation in Albania would change after the "intervention of revisionist and imperialist forces"; he had also allegedly "spewed venom on the cooperative system in general" and "listened to news broadcasts from foreign radio stations and commented on them, approved of anti-communist books and distributed them, etc." According to this account Father Kurti was convicted in a group trial at an open hearing in the village of Gurrez, at which he and his co-defendants received "the punishment they deserved" (unspecified).

Amnesty International notes that the account in *Studime Historike* makes no mention of charges of espionage against Father Kurti. Nor does it offer an explanation for the lapse of time—which appears inconsistent with Albanian judicial practice — between his arrest in 1967 and his execution, allegedly in 1970.

Although organized religion has been suppressed in Albania since 1967, the official press has continued to publish articles denouncing the persistence of religious practices and customs. On 26 October 1983, however, an article in *Zeri i Popullit* denied that religious believers had been persecuted in Albania and said that religion had not been fought "with laws and state decrees or with restrictions and force". Religious faith had been opposed with arguments, it asserted. It quoted a saying attributed to Enver Hoxha that "to believe or not to believe is each person's right". However, the article failed to refer to the fact that public worship continues to be banned and that all religious communities have been suppressed.

16

Restrictions on freedom of movement

The Constitution does not guarantee freedom of movement, and, apart from official delegations and a limited number of students studying abroad, Albanian citizens are almost never permitted to leave their country. The frontiers are heavily guarded and people who try to leave the country without official permission risk being shot by border guards, or long years of imprisonment if they are captured.

Kostas Moukas, a former prisoner, who succeeded in crossing the border from Albania into Greece in early 1983, has alleged that in December 1982 he saw the blood-stained corpse of a 19-year-old ethnic Greek from the village of Frashtani, who on official orders was being dragged behind a tractor through the villages of the Dropull area in the south of Albania, as an example to deter other would-be emigrants. The teenager, Spyridon Kokkoris, had allegedly been shot the previous day by border guards while attempting to flee into Greece.

Those who are arrested while trying to leave the country illegally face conviction under Article 47 of the Criminal Code (Article 64 of the previous code), dealing with "treason". Paragraph 11 of Article 47 makes "flight from the state" and "refusal to return to the fatherland on the part of a person sent on service or allowed temporarily to leave the state" an offence punishable by not less than 10 years' imprisonment or death. Prison sentences imposed during the 1950s and 1960s under Article 64 on people convicted of attempting to flee the country have varied, in the cases known to Amnesty International, between 12 and 25 years. Similarly high sentences have reportedly been imposed in the 1970s. However, Amnesty International knows of two cases in which the accused received sentences below the minimum provided for by the law. In one case this appears to have been because the accused—who received a six-year sentence—was a minor. In the other, where the accused reportedly received a five-year sentence, the charges may possibly have been brought under the milder Article 127 of the Criminal Code, dealing with "illegal crossing of the border", rather than Article 47. Former prisoners of conscience convicted of "flight from the state" about whom Amnesty International knows include a craftsman from central Albania arrested in 1963 while trying to cross the border and subsequently sentenced by a military court to 18 years' imprisonment.

Arrest, trial and sentencing

Arrest and pre-trial investigation

Under Articles 49 and 50 of the Code of Criminal Procedure of 1980 only a court or investigating authority can order arrest and custody, and when it is the investigating authority who makes this order it must be approved by a procurator before it may be carried out. The arrest warrant must state the offence with which the suspect is charged and the reasons for making the arrest. The following constitute grounds for arrest: if the offence in question is punishable by imprisonment; if the accused is liable to avoid investigation, trial or punishment, or to hamper the investigation; if the accused is caught in the act of committing the offence, or if the court and investigating authority consider the arrest to be necessary "because of the social danger represented by the act and the accused". The above provisions, however, may be overridden in "exceptional cases" (unspecified) and a person held for up to 14 days without charge, under Article 47 of the Code of Criminal Procedure.

In addition, investigating authorities, officials of the Department of Internal Affairs and the commands of military units are authorized to detain a person without a warrant in certain circumstances (for example, when that person is caught in the act of committing an offence) for up to 72 hours. The local procurator must be informed immediately of the detention and may order the detainee's release if it is established that there are no grounds for detention (Articles 68 and 70 of the Code of Criminal Procedure).

The law provides for few legal safeguards for the accused during investigation proceedings. According to Article 76 of the Code of Criminal Procedure, once the order to charge someone has been issued, the person charged must be informed of this within 24 hours and must be interrogated by the investigator within the following 24 hours. A report is made of the interrogation which the detainee is entitled to read; he may request that it be supplemented or corrected. If experts are consulted in the course of an investigation the detainee may request their exclusion, designate others, and request additional questions to be asked. There is no specific provision, however, for the right of the detainee to call witnesses for the defence, although Article 14 states that participants in penal proceedings have the right "to make requests and to produce explanations, as well as to make complaints against the activities or decisions of the court and the investigator". Equally, there are no provisions granting the accused the right to be visited by members of his family or to receive letters, clothes or food from them during investigation proceedings.

Under Article 61, investigations into crimes against the state and certain other offences must be completed within three months. Exceptionally, the investigating authority may, with the approval of the district procurator, extend the investigation by up to one month, but must obtain the approval of the Procurator General for any further extension. No maximum time-limit is laid down. In Amnesty International's experience, most investigations of political offences in recent years have been completed within three to four months, although there have been cases when they have taken up to 13 months. Investigations have usually been carried out by investigators of the Department of Internal Affairs (police headquarters) of the district capital. *Sigurimi* officials are frequently reported to have taken part in investigations.

Almost all former political prisoners who have given testimonies to Amnesty International have stated that during investigation they were held in solitary confinement, often in small, dark basement cells. In many cases they apparently had to sleep either on the cell floor or on boards, with blankets but no mattress. They have complained that they were given very little to eat and were allowed little or no exercise. As a general rule they were denied access to their families and to legal counsel (see below), and were interrogated daily for long periods. Several have stated that they were interrogated at night and deprived of sleep.

An account of such experiences was published in the London *Sunday Times* newspaper on 7 July 1974. It was by Joseph Valyrakis, a Greek citizen who escaped to Albania in 1972 after taking part in the resistance movement against the military regime in Greece. He said that after swimming from Corfu to the Albanian coast in May 1972 he was arrested and taken to the police station of the town of Sarande: "After a week they moved me to a cell in the basement.... It was abominable. I was not allowed to wear shoes or a belt. There were lots of rats and cockroaches. The cell had only a small window with a tight net of bars. Every day they interrogated me for hours." In July 1972 he was sentenced to three years' imprisonment for entering Albania illegally, but was pardoned and released in December 1973.

Ill-treatment and torture

Article 7 of the Code of Criminal Procedure prohibits the "use of physical or psychological force, as well as of other such measures" during investigation proceedings. This provision is reinforced by Article 115 of the Criminal Code which makes the extraction of confessions by force an offence punishable by up to eight years' imprisonment.

Nevertheless, the majority of testimonies by former political prisoners received by Amnesty International have alleged that during investigation the accused was beaten, and the available evidence indicates that investigators have readily resorted to beatings and other forms of coercion, such as threats, in order to obtain a detainee's confession or collaboration. Those former political prisoners who have said they were not ill-treated during investigation had in almost all cases been arrested while attempting to leave the country illegally, so that there was no need for a "confession".

At the same time, Amnesty International notes that many of the worst abuses in the period up to the late 1960s appear to have ceased in recent years, or have been alleged only rarely. Reports from the earlier period referred, for example, to prisoners being tortured by suspension from a pole, by immersion for several hours at a time in a cistern of cold water, or by having hot eggs placed under their armpits. One former prisoner arrested at the beginning of the 1960s alleged that his body had been burned with hot irons and that wood splinters had been forced under his nails.

Since the 1970s, the allegations of ill-treatment made to Amnesty International have usually involved beatings. The following allegations were made by ethnic Greeks. With the exception of Zissis Angelis and Spyros Lekas (the latter was not brought to trial), each was arrested on charges of having engaged in "anti-state agitation and propaganda" and after investigation was convicted and sentenced to between six and eight years' imprisonment.

● Zissis Angelis, born in 1958 in Kullurica, Sarande district, was arrested in 1974 when he was 16 on charges of having planned to flee the country with a group of other people. While detained for investigation in Sarande he was allegedly confined in a damp cell, deprived of sleep and forced to stand for hours at a time. He has also alleged that he was beaten with a length of

rubber hose filled with gravel and that he was suspended over a
cistern of water and threatened with being dropped into it.

● Spyros Lekas, born in 1937 in Gline, Gjirokaster district,
described his treatment in Vlore investigation centre after his
arrest on 19 January 1982 as follows:

"They handcuffed my hands behind my back. They took me
to prison and put me in a cell 2m by 2½m, without furniture.
It had a cement floor. There they freed my hands and
removed my shoes, belt—everything except my vest, shirt
and trousers. I could go to the toilet twice a day, at 6.00am
and 6.00pm.

"After a while they handcuffed me again and took me to a
room where there were three policemen. One of them, who
was seated, wrote down my answers. Another came up to
me and said: 'What have you spoken against the Albanians
and Hoxha since 1967?' 'I've said nothing. I have worked to
raise my children.' 'No', they said, and the policeman from
Gline hit my face with the side of his hand and kicked my
legs . . . . The other caught me by the throat and asked:
'Why did you say that maize bread is bad and that we
should have wheat bread?' I tried to say 'I never said that'
but he punched me in the jaw. I spat blood from my tongue.
My teeth ached.

"They asked me other questions and continued to beat
me . . . After one question, one of the policemen struck me
three times in the chest. I fell to the ground. They threw a
glass of water in my face. They pulled me up and forced me
to stand. [He was forced to adopt an uncomfortable posture
and to stand like this for long periods] . . . I didn't admit
anything for three days . . . The policeman from Gline
grabbed me by the shirt and shook me, banging my head and
back against the wall . . . .

"On the fourth day I began to confess to what they had
accused me of. I said 'Whatever is written against me by my
Albanian and Greek "friends" I will sign. I beg you not to
torture me, I am not an animal . . .'."

Spyros Lekas was released after six days after signing
statements that he and his two nephews had criticized the
Albanian authorities and political system. All three fled to
Greece in April 1982.

● In a sworn statement made in Athens in November 1983,
Kostas Moukas, born in 1961 in Zervat, Gjirokaster district,
stated that he had been arrested on 14 August 1981 while

serving as a conscript. He alleged that he had been frequently beaten while detained for investigation in Gjirokaster and Tirane. He named the official in charge of the investigation in Gjirokaster as Kasem Berberi.

After Kostas Moukas had hit an interrogator he was transferred to Tirane investigation centre at the end of September 1981. Here he was allegedly given repeated electric shocks in the period from early November to the beginning of December. (This is the only allegation of electric shock torture in Albania received by Amnesty International in recent years, although two former political prisoners have claimed that they were tortured by this method in 1958 and 1961 respectively.)

● Evangelos Gribouras, born in 1959 in Cuke, Sarande district, was serving as a military conscript when he was arrested and detained for investigation in Gjirokaster in May 1980. He, too, named Kasem Berberi as the official in charge of the investigation. He said that during the initial phase of his investigation he was interrogated continually at various times of the day and night in a special cell, where he was bound, handcuffed, to a chair fixed to the floor. Several times, he said, he was beaten to the point of fainting, whereupon cold water was thrown over him. According to his testimony, he eventually signed a "confession" which he had not read.

● Ilias Fanis, born in 1957 in Finiq, Sarande district, was apparently arrested in May 1977, after Tryfon Toska, a local investigating official, had denounced him as an enemy of the state at a public meeting. He was not ill-treated during the first few days of his detention but was put in a cell with a man whom he suspected of being an *agent provocateur*. Several days later, after he had refused to collaborate with the police as an informer, he was allegedly punched in the face and subsequently moved to solitary confinement in a cell "with only a hole for light". He was also allegedly threatened with torture by electric shock.

(Kostas Moukas, Evangelos Gribouras and Ilias Fanis fled to Greece after having been released early under the amnesty of November 1982.)

Although the above testimonies are all by ethnic Greeks, accounts by other former prisoners indicate that the ill-treatment alleged is not reserved for this minority, but may be applied to any Albanian citizen suspected of political offences. For instance, a former political prisoner who was detained for investigation in Tepelene in 1972 has stated that he was held in a dark basement cell measuring 3m by 3m which had no outside window. During this period, he said, he was frequently beaten, sometimes with a length of rubber hose filled with gravel. Another former political prisoner who was detained in Tirane's investigation centre in 1979 has alleged that he was on several occasions severely beaten with a rubber truncheon while he was handcuffed. Both former prisoners have a Muslim background.

Indictment

Article 102 of the Code of Penal Procedure lays down that an accused must be informed when an investigation has been concluded and allowed to examine the materials of the case. The accused is entitled to ask for supplementary investigative activity to be undertaken. The procedure then is for the investigator to draft the indictment, a copy of which is to be given to the accused—if necessary, in translation.

The procurator may choose to take part in the investigation, in which case it may not be concluded without his consent. If he discovers violations of the law he may submit a protest to superior officials. Similarly, defendants may appeal to the head of the district investigative office against the activities of investigators who violate or limit their rights.

In practice, however, there appear to be few or no checks on the powers of investigators entrusted with political cases. Moreover, Amnesty International knows of no instance in which a political prisoner was allowed to examine the full materials of his case—they tend to be shown only a copy of the indictment. Joseph Valyrakis (see above) claimed that he was given the text of his indictment but that this was in Albanian only (which, being Greek, he did not understand). When another former political prisoner, Vanghelis Kazandzis, protested during his trial in August 1980 that he had not been allowed to see the materials of his case he was reprimanded by the procurator, who accused him of trying to slander socialist justice. Similarly, Ilias Fanis (see above), who was tried by the district court of Sarande in August 1977, had reportedly been given a copy of the indictment but had not seen the full materials of his case which were at the disposal of the President of the court.

Defence

Legislation was passed in 1946, 1950, 1953 and 1961 on the status of lawyers and the exercise of their profession. Under these laws they were grouped in collectives or "colleges" supervised by the Ministry of Justice. In political cases the possibilities of defending clients were extremely limited—indeed lawyers were required by law to inform on their clients and apparently might even be called to give evidence against them.

Article 16 of Decree No. 1601 of 1953 "Concerning lawyers" stipulated:

"The lawyer is obliged to preserve professional secrecy. Nevertheless, the lawyer is obliged to notify the state authorities of information of which he has come to learn because of his profession when this is connected with activities which constitute crimes against the state defined in Articles 64 to 75 and 83 of the Criminal Code. Lawyers may be called as witnesses on matters about which they have learned in the course of the exercise of their profession on occasions defined in procedural provisions."

Law No. 3350 of 1961 contained similar provisions, but did not refer to the possibility of lawyers being called as witnesses. These laws were superseded in 1967 by Decree No. 4277.

The above provisions doubtless explain the scepticism expressed by former political prisoners about the ability of lawyers to defend their interests. One former prisoner told Amnesty International that throughout his trial in 1963 his lawyer did not utter a word. Another, tried in early 1967, was reportedly informed at the close of investigation proceedings that he had the right to engage a lawyer; he declined to do so, he said, since he did not feel that it would help him, and moreover he did not have the money to pay the fees. Nonetheless, he was defended by a court-appointed lawyer whom he had not seen till his trial. This lawyer reportedly restricted his defence to a recommendation that the court impose a milder sentence than that demanded by the procurator, arguing that a heavy sentence would only embitter the accused and harden him in his hostility to the state and Party.

On 20 June 1967 Decree No. 4277 "Concerning the Creation of Legal Aid Bureaux" was introduced; this annulled all earlier legislation on lawyers and effectively abolished the institution of advocacy. Instead, it created legal aid bureaux attached to district People's Courts, under the jurisdiction of the Supreme Court; these bureaux employ legal advisers appointed (and dismissed) by the President of the Supreme Court. Under this decree, legal advice was not generally available to defendants and it was the court, rather than the accused, that decided whether legal advice was necessary, and appointed the adviser.

The provisions of the current Code of Criminal Procedure, which came into force in April 1980, are similar as regards the

24

defendant's right of defence to those of Decree No. 4277.
Although Article 8 of the Code states that "the defendant enjoys
the right of defence throughout penal proceedings" the two
following articles make it clear that the word "defence" does not
imply the automatic right to the services of a legal adviser, which
is termed "special defence". It is compulsory for a defendant to
have a (court-appointed) legal adviser only if he is under the age
of 18 or if "because of physical or psychological deficiencies he
cannot assure his right to defence". If the defendant is a foreign
citizen and requests a legal adviser the court must designate one.
Otherwise a legal adviser is designated only if "the court deems it
necessary because of the nature of the case or because of other
circumstances". Moreover, even in those cases where it is
compulsory for the accused to have a legal adviser, he is defended
by the latter during the trial only and not throughout penal
proceedings.

Amnesty International knows of only one case since 1967 in
which a court has considered it necessary for an adult Albanian
citizen accused of political offences to be granted the services of a
legal adviser. Even the aid granted to foreigners is liable to be
minimal as is indicated by the case of Joseph Valyrakis (see page
18), who stated that he first met his legal adviser at his trial in July 1972
"She told me I ought to be happy because it was a very minor
charge, considering that they knew I was in fact a foreign agent
and should get 25 years in prison."

Trial

Political offences, like most other offences, are initially tried by
people's courts at district level and appeals are heard by the
Supreme Court. However, the President of the Supreme Court
may request that "important cases" be tried by the Supreme
Court. Cases heard in the first instance are tried by one
professional judge and two lay assessors, and on appeal by three
professional judges. Offences committed by military personnel,
including conscripts, are tried by military benches (at both district
court and Supreme Court levels).

Article 103 of the Constitution states: "The Court administers
justice independently; it decides on the basis of the law alone and
renders its judgment in the name of the people." Article 4 of the
Law on Judicial Organization of 1968, however, contradicts this
principle, stressing the subordination of courts to Party policy: "In
their activity, people's courts are guided by Party policy. In
carrying out their duties they are strongly supported by the
working masses and are subject to their criticism and control."

Trial is open, except when it is deemed necessary to safeguard state secrets, when sexual crimes are being tried or the defendant is under 16 (Article 135 of the Code of Criminal Procedure). Indeed both the Constitution and the Code of Criminal Procedure stress the educational role of open trials, and to enhance this role the court is authorized, if it wishes, to hold the trial not in a courtroom but "in work centres, in city wards or in villages in the presence of working people".

This emphasis on the "educational role" of the judicial process has often resulted in what are effectively political "show trials". The active participants in such trials are generally limited to the judges and lay assessors, the defendant and witnesses for the prosecution. The procurator is entitled to participate in trials, but his presence is not obligatory unless the court specifically orders it. In a number of cases known to Amnesty International no procurator was present, and, after the judge had read the indictment to the accused and examined the defendant and witnesses, proceedings were closed with the verdict and sentence. While the available information suggests that major political trials of senior state officials are closed, most political trials of which Amnesty International knows (in which the defendants have been ordinary citizens) have been open—although in two cases the President of the court reportedly excluded the public after the defendant had attempted to refute the charges against him. Trials have generally been concluded within a day, and Amnesty International knows of no political trials in which the defendant was acquitted.

Sentencing

Article 16 of the Criminal Code describes the penalty for an offence as a "means of coercion of a political and an ideological character used by the socialist state in the class struggle. The penalty is a powerful weapon of the dictatorship of the proletariat in the struggle against its enemies to defend and strengthen the socialist social order."

The aim of imposing the penalty is said to be "to prevent further criminal activity by the culprit and to educate him to become useful to society. The penalty also has the purpose of contributing to the education of other citizens in a spirit of respect for socialist legality."

Imprisonment

Apart from the death penalty, the most severe form of punishment is imprisonment, which may last from one month to a maximum of

25 years and is served either in prisons or in "centres for re-education through work" — in other words, forced labour camps.

Political offenders face severe penalties. Almost all offences against the state are punishable by not less than 10 years' imprisonment or death. The exceptions to this concern the less serious forms of "anti-state agitation and propaganda" (Article 55.1) and "incitement to hatred or discord between nationalities and races" (Article 56)—both punishable by three to 10 years' imprisonment.

The information available to Amnesty International indicates that many Albanian political prisoners are serving long prison sentences and that these sentences have in some cases been increased by further sentences imposed on them in prison. In 1984 Amnesty International knew the names of over 140 political prisoners who were said to have been serving sentences in the 1970s and early 1980s of over 10 years' imprisonment. Many of them had reportedly received prison sentences of up to 20 years. Information provided by a former prisoner released under the amnesty of November 1982 suggests that approximately 800 prisoners—two thirds of the political prisoners in Spac at that time—were serving sentences of over eight years' imprisonment.

Internment

In addition to prison sentences, courts may impose supplementary penalties, including a ban on exercising a specific activity or trade, the deprivation of voting rights, and banishment or internment for a term of one to five years. **Banishment** is defined as the "removal of the convict from his place of residence with or without a prohibition on his staying in one or more [other] specified places" and **internment** as "the obligation of a convict to remain in a specified place". The deprivation of voting rights and internment, which is served after the expiry of the prison sentence, appear to be the supplementary penalties most frequently applied to political prisoners.

A person who is interned is generally sent to live and work on a state farm or state enterprise away from home. Internees may not leave, even for short periods, without permission from the local police. This has reportedly meant that a number of internees have had to wait for several days for permission to seek urgent medical treatment in nearby towns.

Administrative internment

Internment may also be imposed as an administrative measure, that is, without charge or trial. The first decree regulating administrative internment appears to date back to 1949. The currently valid regulations on administrative internment (and banishment) were set down in Decree no. 5912 of 26 June 1979. Under its terms the "Internment and Banishment Commission"— composed of the Deputy Chairperson of the Council of Ministers, the Minister of the Interior, the President of the Supreme Court and the Procurator General—may order the internment or banishment of people who "represent a danger to the social system". No indication is given of the criteria used by the Commission in imposing such a punishment. The decree refers to the time-limits specified in the Criminal Code (one to five years), but states that when internment or banishment are imposed administratively, they may be revoked, curtailed or prolonged (for unspecified periods) as the Commission sees fit.

Administrative internment may also be imposed on people who have not committed any offence and who do not themselves necessarily constitute any "danger to the social system": Article 2 of the decree states that relatives of people who have fled from Albania or who have gone into hiding inside the country may be administratively interned.

Amnesty International has information on a number of cases in which internment has been imposed as a supplementary penalty by courts; it has also learned of cases in which individuals and whole families have been administratively interned. However, it has only fragmentary information about how the measure is applied. Administrative internment is alleged to have been used extensively—and the fact that it was the subject of legislation in the 1940s, 1950s, 1960s and again in 1979 indicates that it has been in regular use over the past 40 years.

Review and release procedures

Appeal

A defendant (or a procurator) may appeal to the Supreme Court against judgments delivered by district courts. The appeal must be filed within five days of the announcement of the judgment and must be examined by the Supreme Court within one month. (The Supreme Court examines all death sentences within 10 days, whether or not an appeal has been filed.) The President of the Supreme Court and the Procurator General may at any time file a "request for the protection of legality"; the case will then be examined by the Supreme Court or the plenum of the appropriate section of the Supreme Court. The information available to Amnesty International suggests that most political prisoners do not appeal against their sentences, believing it to be useless. One former political prisoner reported that after his conviction he was visited in his cell by a legal adviser, who told him that his parents wished to file an appeal, but that he had sent the man away. Another explained his failure to appeal as follows: "If the wolf-cub bites me, do I complain to the big wolf?"

Amnesty International knows of only two cases of political prisoners' sentences having been reduced: two death sentences which were reportedly commuted to 20 and 25 years' imprisonment.

Early conditional release

Early release on parole is no longer possible in Albania. The Criminal Code of 1952 contained provisions for the early conditional release of prisoners whose conduct and work showed that they had reformed. When the current Criminal Code was introduced in 1977 it contained similar provisions under Article 39, and several former political prisoners have told Amnesty International that they had obtained early release by exceeding the set work norms.

However, Article 39 and the related provisions of the Code of

Criminal Procedure were annulled in March 1981. Amnesty International has not heard of any official explanation for this change.

Pardon

Article 77 of the Constitution empowers the Presidium of the People's Assembly to grant full or partial pardon. Before 1967 prisoners, their relatives, friends and lawyers were entitled to apply for pardon directly to the Presidium (government and state agencies could also apply for them to be pardoned). Since July 1967, only people sentenced to death (or their families) have this right. In all other cases, a pardon can only be granted if this has been proposed by an official body such as the Council of Ministers, the courts and the procuracy, or by officials of the Department of Internal Affairs—who make their proposals on their own initiative or at the request of the prisoners or their families.

Amnesty International knows of only two former prisoners of conscience, both foreign citizens, who were pardoned and released early.

Amnesty

To Amnesty International's knowledge, there have been four amnesties affecting convicted prisoners since the end of the Second World War, in 1957, 1959, 1962 and 1982. There were also amnesties in 1956 and 1959 for people who had fled abroad and wished to return to Albania.

The amnesties of 1957, 1959 and 1962 were broadly similar in their provisions for convicted prisoners. People sentenced to up to five years' imprisonment (three years in the case of the 1957 amnesty) were released, as were people convicted of military offences, minors, pregnant women, women over 45 or with young children, and men over 60. Those sentenced to over five years' imprisonment (or three in the case of the 1957 amnesty) had a part of the remainder of their sentences reduced.

These provisions applied also to people convicted of certain political offences, such as "anti-state agitation", "sabotage" or "conspiracy". However, given the high minimum sentences prescribed in law for these offences it must be assumed that the majority would not have been freed but would have benefited only by a reduction of sentence. Certain categories of political offences, however, were excluded (including espionage and terrorism), as were grave economic offences and violent offences (including murder and robbery with violence). ·

Amnesty International does not know how many convicted prisoners benefited from these various amnesties.

The People's Assembly is empowered to grant amnesty under Article 67 of the current Constitution. Since its promulgation in 1976 there has been only one amnesty, which was technically termed a "pardon" since it was in fact decreed by the Presidium of the People's Assembly. This decree, which marked the 70th anniversary of national independence, came into force on 15 November 1982 and was similar in many aspects to the previous amnesties. However, although it applied to a wide range of ordinary criminal offences, it benefited only two categories of political prisoner:

— Those sentenced to up to eight years' imprisonment for anti--state agitation and propaganda under Article 55.1 of the current Criminal Code were released — those convicted under Article 55.2 (i.e. "anti-state agitation and propaganda" with "especially grave consequences") were excluded.

— People convicted under Article 47 (dealing with "treason"), paragraph 11 ("flight from the state"), had the remainder of their sentence reduced by one quarter.

The amnesty also covered people detained for investigation on corresponding charges, and people who had committed such offences up to the time the decree came into force. The amnesty did not apply to prisoners convicted of all other crimes against the state (or recidivists), except for those who had only a year left of their sentence to serve: they were released.

The Albanian embassy in Vienna was reported to have stated at the time that this amnesty could affect several thousand people, but no official figures were published. Amnesty International does not know how many political prisoners benefited. A former prisoner who was himself released under the amnesty told the organization that some 360 political prisoners detained in Spac were released—almost a third of the prisoners held there at that time. After the amnesty was announced, prisoners who were to be released were reportedly kept apart before their departure from Spac to protect them from the despair and anger of those who were to remain behind. Another former prisoner who benefited by the amnesty gave Amnesty International the names of 13 political prisoners in Ballsh prison who, he said, were released under its provisions, but it is possible that the number was greater.

The death penalty

Under the Criminal Code death sentences may be imposed for 34 offences, 12 of them political and 11 military. The death penalty may be imposed in peacetime for a number of non-violent political offences, including "flight from the state" (Article 47.11), "anti-state agitation and propaganda" when this has "specially grave consequences" (Article 55.2), "creation of a counter-revolutionary organization or participation in it" (Article 57), and "concealment of a person who commits a crime against the state" in "specially serious circumstances" (Article 59).

Offenders who have not completed their 18th year and women offenders who are pregnant when the crime is committed or when they come to trial are exempt from the death penalty. A death sentence is not carried out if a woman offender is found to be pregnant at the time scheduled for execution.

The Supreme Court examines all death sentences within 10 days of the conviction in a court of first instance, regardless of whether the defendant has filed an appeal. If the sentence is confirmed, the defendant may appeal for clemency to the Presidium of the People's Assembly, which must in any case examine and approve all death sentences before they can be carried out (Article 186 of the Code of Criminal Procedure).

A Decree on the Application of Sentences of 1962 states that a death sentence is carried out by officials of the Ministry of Internal Affairs by shooting, unless the court orders the prisoner to be hanged instead. A procurator, doctor and a secretary are present at the execution. In the past executions could be in public, but the law does not specify whether this is so still.

No official figures on death sentences have been made public and there is little recent information available about the death penalty in Albania. Most such information concerns reports of the execution of senior party and state officials following purges. For instance, it was reported that Liri Gega, a member of the Party's Central Committee, was executed in 1956 after being accused of having been a Titoist agent, allegedly following her capture while trying to cross the border into Yugoslavia. In 1961 the commander of Albania's naval forces, Rear-Admiral Teme Sejko, was reportedly tried and executed. The Minister of Defence, General Beqir Balluku, and a number of his supporters were reported to have been executed in the mid-1970s. In November 1982 Enver Hoxha announced the arrest of Fecor Shehu, Minister of the Interior until 1982, and of a "group of plotters" linked with him. In 1983 sources outside Albania claimed that Fecor Shehu had been executed together with Kadri Hazbiu, former Defence Minister, and two other senior officials. Albanian diplomatic representatives in Vienna were reported to have declined to comment on these allegations but to have confirmed that legal proceedings against "traitors" had taken place.

Yugoslav sources have claimed that the provisions of a decree of 26 February 1951 "On the prosecution and trial of the activities of terrorist organizations and terrorist acts against representatives of the people's authorities and of political and other organizations of the Albanian People's Republic" are still in force. This decree, which was introduced in exceptional circumstances, at a time when Great Britain and the United States had organized the parachuting of armed Albanian insurgents into the country, required that the investigation of such offences be terminated within 10 days and that the indictment be given to the accused only one day before trial. The accused was denied the right to appear at the trial or to appeal against the verdict. In cases where the death sentence was imposed, this was to be carried out immediately after the verdict was announced. Amnesty International does not know if this legislation is still in force, but the reported summary trial and execution of four political prisoners in Spac labour camp on 24 May 1973, four days after they had led a protest by fellow-prisoners, suggests that it had not at that time been annulled (see below under Spac labour camp, page 41).

Political imprisonment

The late 1940s and the 1950s saw the mass imprisonment and internment of opponents or presumed opponents of communist rule. Thousands were sent to do forced labour on major industrial and agricultural projects, including the construction of roads, railways, airfields and factories, and work on land drainage and irrigation.*

Amnesty International's information primarily concerns political imprisonment in the 1970s and early 1980s. However, it has received accounts by former political prisoners referring to earlier periods. Among these is an account by the Albanian poet and scholar Arshi Pipa, who was a political prisoner from 1946 to 1956 and later fled the country. In appendices to his collection of poems *Libri i Burgut* (The Prison Notebook) published in the USA in 1959, he relates that he was first sent to prison in Durres, where he and other political prisoners worked building roads. In July 1948 he was moved to a labour camp at Vlocisht (the mortality rate at this camp was so high that it was known as a "death camp"). In 1950 he was transferred to the prison of Gjirokaster, where political prisoners were detained underground in cellars. After nearly two years he was sent to Burrel labour camp.

*In December 1955 the Secretary-General of the United Nations and the Director General of the International Labour Office presented to the United Nations Economic and Social Council a report submitted by the United States Government, "Evidence of the Existence of Forced Labour in Albania", together with the summaries of 13 affidavits made by former political prisoners or internees who had fled their country.

The report listed some 40 political prisons, labour camps and places of internment which it said had been in operation in Albania at various times between 1944 and 1954. An estimated 80,000 men, women and children had spent time in one or other of these places and some 16,000 were said to have perished in them. (Under Article 6 of the Criminal Code of 1952 the lower age limit for penal responsibility was set at 14 years, but in the case of crimes against the state this limit was lowered to 12 years.) Among the figures cited by the report was that in a statement reportedly made by the Director of the Statistical Bureau in the State

Another former political prisoner has told Amnesty International that after his arrest in 1950 he was sent to camp No. 301 to work on the construction of a meat factory in Tirane. In 1952 camp 301 was moved to Berat, where a military airfield was being built. From 1954 to 1960 he successively worked in labour camps where prisoners were engaged in draining marshes (in Skrofotine, near Vlore), digging irrigation channels (Shtyllas-Fier district) and building dams (at Hajmel on the River Drin near Shkoder). He also worked as a carpenter in Shkoder prison, where prisoners produced furniture for the army.

According to testimony given to Amnesty International by people who served political sentences during the 1960s, political prisoners during this period were employed on the following projects, among others: camps 303 and 305, with a total of some 800 prisoners, worked on two building sites near Tirane from 1962 to 1964; from 1964 to 1968 camp 303 was employed in the construction of a caustic soda factory in Vlore and cement factories in Elbasan and Fush-Kruje (both political prisoners and ordinary criminals worked on the latter site). In the late 1960s camp 303 began work in the copper mines of Spac (Mirdite district). In 1967 some 250 political prisoners in camp 309 were employed in the construction of a factory in Lac and in draining the marshes north of the town of Vlore. In 1972 camp 309 was moved to Ballsh (Fier district), where an oil refinery was being built.

Political imprisonment since the beginning of the 1970s

Political offenders sentenced to imprisonment serve their sentences either in prisons or in corrective labour camps. Both these

---

Prosecutor's Office (who fled Albania late in 1948) that at the end of 1947 there were some 18,000 political prisoners, in addition to those interned in labour camps. The report estimated that in 1954 there were some 10,000 political prisoners serving sentences in prisons and another 10,000 to 15,000 detained in labour camps. It noted that internment had first been introduced in the late 1940s and that "As a rule, people from the north are sent to camps in the south, particularly in Tepelene, Himare, Berat etc; while people from the south are interned at Kruje, Burrel, Kamze, Valias, Cerrik and other places in the north." The report said that as projects were completed, certain camps had been closed down and others opened up. Thus, for example, early in 1952 most of the inmates of the camp in Valias were transferred to work on the construction of an oil refinery at Cerrik near Elbasan, and in 1952-1953 some 1,500 forced labourers were moved from various camps to Ura Vajgurore and Berat to help in the construction of a military airfield.

institutions fall under the jurisdiction of the Ministry of Internal Affairs and are administered by its employees. The Procuracy is responsible for ensuring that legality is respected within prisons and camps.

Decree No. 3584 of 12 November 1962, on the "Application of Sentences", indicates that prisons are regarded as a severer form of punishment than corrective labour camps. Convicted prisoners are sent to a prison if they commit "grave or systematic violations" of camp regulations, or if their detention in a labour camp "represents a risk" or if they are not able to work because of their physical health. Decree No. 3584 refers to separate sets of regulations for prisons and corrective labour camps, but these do not appear to be generally available to the public.

Before trial (and sometimes for a short period after conviction) political prisoners are generally held in the police headquarters of the capital of the district in which they were arrested. In some cases, however, they have been sent to the investigative section of Tirane prison. After trial, most political prisoners are temporarily transferred to another section of Tirane prison for a period ranging from several days to a month before being moved to the prison or labour camp where they are to serve their sentences.

Adult male political prisoners serve their sentences apart from ordinary criminals. Male political prisoners under 18 and female political prisoners serve their sentences together with ordinary criminals.

Although prisoners are all, formally, subject to the same regime, ex-political prisoners have reported that in practice prisoners who cooperate with the prison authorities and are willing to inform on fellow-inmates receive privileged treatment, including in some cases being allowed conjugal visits.

Former political prisoners have, without exception, described their treatment and conditions as harsh. Their accounts have frequently included the allegation that if a prisoner dies while serving his sentence, his relatives are informed of his death but may not collect his remains until the date of the expiry of his sentence. Amnesty International has not been able to verify this allegation but it appears to be a commonly held belief among prisoners.

Prisons and camps

All male former political prisoners who have served sentences since the 1970s and who have testified to Amnesty International were detained in either Spac or Ballsh labour camps, or, in a few cases, in Burrel prison. Female prisoners reportedly serve their sentences in Kosove (Elbasan district) and men under 18 in Tarovic (Lezhe district). There have also been reports that a number of political prisoners serve their sentences with ordinary criminals in Tirane prison and in Bulqize labour camp (Diber district), where chromium is mined, but Amnesty International does not know of any specific prisoners who have been sent to these two institutions. Various emigre sources have referred to still other prisons and camps where political prisoners are alleged to have been held.

Number of political prisoners

In view of the extreme official secrecy surrounding political imprisonment and the lack of any published official figures, Amnesty International cannot accurately assess how many political prisoners are detained in Albania. It has in recent years received the names of almost 400 political prisoners who were serving sentences in the 1970s and early 1980s, and the limited details available indicate that many were prisoners of conscience. However, this figure represents only a fraction of all political prisoners. Former political prisoners who have served sentences in the past 10 years have put the number of Albanian political prisoners in Ballsh labour camp before November 1982 at approximately 1,200 (plus a small number of foreign prisoners). Similar figures have been given for Spac labour camp, although it appears that in the latter half of the 1960s there were fewer prisoners (around 500) and that subsequently the numbers rose at times to 1,700. The population of both camps was reduced after the 1982 amnesty but Amnesty International has received allegations that since then there have been further arrests of people considered to have supported senior government officials disgraced and arrested in 1982.

Any accurate figure for the number of political prisoners would have to take into account not only those in Spac and Ballsh but others in Burrel prison (allegedly some 300 inmates), in Tarovic and Kosove, as well as prisoners held for investigation, others temporarily detained in Tirane prison pending transfer, those serving supplementary sentences of internment, and individuals and families administratively interned for political reasons.

Spac labour camp 303

Spac labour camp for political prisoners is in Mirdite district, a major copper-producing region, and prisoners in the camp are employed in the mining of pyrites, from which copper is extracted.

The mining area lies within the camp itself, which is surrounded by several rows of barbed-wire fencing 3m high, with watchtowers manned by armed guards at regular intervals. The camp's outer perimeter is patrolled by military guards with dogs. At night spotlights are trained on the fences.

The following information about conditions in Spac is based on the testimony of former prisoners.

Prisoners are housed in unheated concrete barracks with some 300-400 prisoners to each unit, divided among 12-15 rooms. They sleep on straw mattresses on three-tier wooden platforms along each side of the room and are provided with two to three blankets, and (since 1975) with sheets, which are changed once a month. There is a separate washroom with showers, but these are apparently frequently out of order and prisoners usually wash at cold taps in the washroom or in the mine galleries, where water is available. In an annexe to the washroom, prisoners can sometimes heat water for cooking or to wash themselves and their clothes. Work uniforms of heavy cotton are issued once a year, helmets every two years and boots every six months.

The daily food ration for prisoners who work is said to be as follows: bread (often made with maize flour)—800-900g; potatoes—245g; sugar—10-25g; jam—150g; oil—15g; meat—30-45g; beans—150g; condensed milk—15g. Prisoners who do not work receive much less. Without exception former prisoners have stated that the food was very poor and the diet seriously deficient in protein, fresh vegetables and fruit. Prisoners commonly suffer a severe loss of weight.

The main meal is usually bread and soup with beans and rice or macaroni. Prisoners supplement these rations with food sent by their families (they may receive up to 10kg a month, but it seems that few receive regular parcels) and with purchases of oil, macaroni, rice and biscuits at the prison canteen (which also sells cigarettes).

The prison has a small infirmary with some 10 beds; both the doctor and dentist are themselves prisoners and can only provide the most basic treatment (dental care is said to be limited to extractions). Prisoners have complained that unless they are running high fevers they are forced to work. Gravely ill prisoners are sent to Tirane prison hospital. Some former prisoners have referred to the problem of mental disturbance and illness among inmates. One prisoner who was detained in Spac in the late 1960s alleged that he had seen mentally ill prisoners throw themselves on the barbed-wire fence surrounding the camp, where they had been shot by guards.

Spac labour camp 303

This plan of Spac labour camp 303 is based on sketches by former prisoners who were there between the mid-1970s and 1982. The camp is said to be ringed by several high barbed-wire fences (see top of page 37).

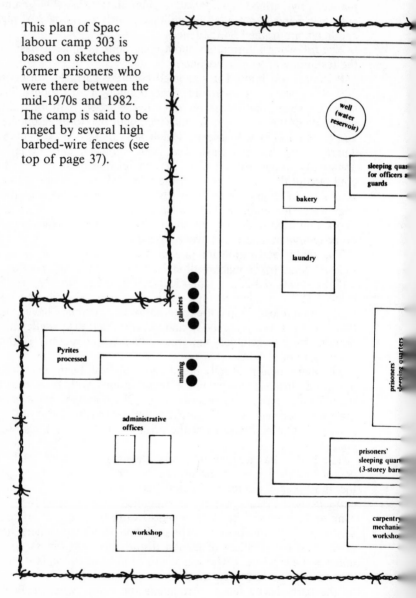

well (water reservoir)

sleeping quar for officers a guards

bakery

laundry

galleries

Pyrites processed

mining

prisoners' sleeping quarters

administrative offices

prisoners' sleeping quart (3-storey barn

workshop

carpentry mechani worksho

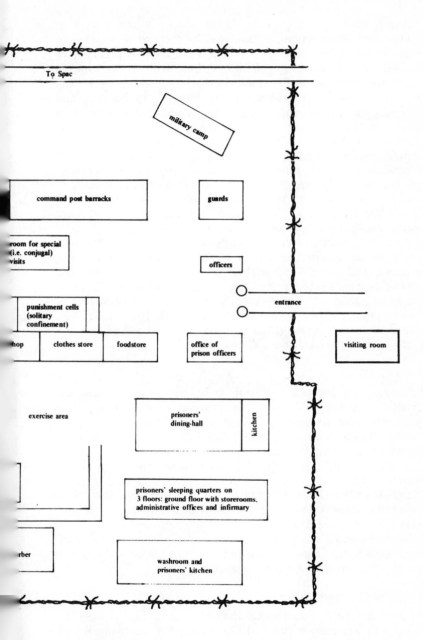

Work

Prisoners work eight hours a day in the mines, six days a week. It is apparently not uncommon, however, for them to be required to work on the seventh day as well. The work consists primarily of opening up and securing galleries, drilling rock to lay charges (these are set off by civilian non-prisoners) and loading the broken rock onto wagons. Work norms are reported to be high and prisoners who fail to achieve them may be required to work extra hours, or be punished by deprivation of visits or solitary confinement. Those who achieve work norms are reportedly paid between two and a half and three leks a day, and most prisoners average about 60 leks a month (the average civilian wage for comparable work is about 480 leks a month). Industrial protection is said to be very poor. A prisoner who was released from Spac in November 1982 stated that towards the end of his time there cotton masks were not replaced when they wore out. Prisoners were told that new machinery using water would be introduced which would render the use of protective masks unnecessary; however, this did not materialize while he was there and thus some prisoners worked without the protection of masks. Lack of industrial safeguards has reportedly led to serious accidents. A former prisoner held in Ballsh in the late 1970s recalled the arrival there of four prisoners from Spac who had become partially paralysed after the collapse of a gallery.

Visits

Prisoners are allowed half-hour visits by relatives once, or sometimes twice, a month. In practice, comparatively few prisoners seem to receive regular visits, either because their families are intimidated or because they lack the necessary time or money to make long journeys.

Visits generally take place in a room outside the camp, in the presence of a guard. Prisoners and visitors are separated by bars. Members of the Greek minority have complained that they were forbidden to speak to their relatives in their mother tongue and were obliged to use Albanian.

Relatives may bring food and clothing for prisoners. The latter may receive any number of letters but may write only two a month. All correspondence is censored.

Education, recreation

Ex-prisoners have reported that they were given regular political lectures by the camp's Political Commissar but the frequency of this form of education appears to have varied considerably.

No vocational training is provided and prisoners are not allowed to study or teach each other foreign languages. There is a library which is said to be stocked almost exclusively with official texts by Party leaders, and prisoners may subscribe to the official daily press. In the evening radio programs are broadcast over a loudspeaker and prisoners may watch television for a few hours. A film is shown once a month. Prisoners are permitted to play dominoes or chess (not cards) and volley-ball. In the past there was reportedly a prisoners' orchestra, but this was banned after a prison riot in 1973.

Discipline and punishments

A prisoner who quarrels with other inmates or with guards, who breaks camp regulations or fails to achieve work norms may be punished in a variety of ways: by deprivation of the right to visits, correspondence or parcels, by being given reduced rations and by solitary confinement in a small, windowless cell known a a *biruce*. The prison authorities may impose the latter punishment for up to one month, which may be extended to three months with the approval of the district procurator. During confinement in the *biruce* prisoners do not work.

A former prisoner has alleged that he was punished by three months' solitary confinement in the early 1980s after he had tattooed an eagle (the Albanian national emblem) without an accompanying communist red star symbol on his body. He said the cell measured no more than 2m by 1.5m. He slept on a mattress and had only one blanket. (Other former prisoners have alleged that they were sometimes forced to sleep on the cell's bare cement floor or were at best given a blanket or board to sleep on.) While undergoing this punishment he was denied letters and visits, received reduced food rations and was allowed only three cigarettes a day, he said.

Another former prisoner detained during the 1970s in Spac alleged that on three occasions guards had stripped him to the waist, tied him to a post and beaten him with a length of rubber hose filled with gravel.

Strikes and violent protests by prisoners in Spac camp

The severity of conditions and treatment in Spac camp have provoked prisoners to engage in strikes and violent protest on at least two occasions, in 1973 and 1978. Both times the protests were ruthlessly suppressed by the authorities and the leaders were executed. The most detailed account received by Amnesty International concerns the events of 1973; it was given by a former prisoner who had participated in the Spac strike that year.

"At 6.30 am on 19 May, as we were about to begin the first shift, we heard guards beating our fellow-prisoners in the camp cells. We demanded that the camp and prison authorities should put an end to this. But our demand was met with threats and blows. We were isolated in a corridor leading out of the camp to where we worked. Soon other prisoners came to our aid and there followed clashes with the guards. After about 20 minutes we forced the guards to withdraw. We then organized a meeting in the camp dining-hall and came to a unanimous decision to seek the help of the United Nations with a view to getting their representatives to intervene on our behalf as soon as possible. We forwarded this request to government representatives in Tirane. This request was repeated in large letters on a cardboard placard . . . .

"Large army and police forces arrived at the camp, together with senior government officials and the Camp Commandant, Muharrem Shehu; the Camp Commissar, Shahin Skura; the head of the Department of Internal Affairs of Mirdite district, Pandi Kita; the Chief Security Officer of Mirdite, Gjergj Zefi; the camp Security Officer, Fejzi Aliaj, and others. They appealed to us over the loudspeaker to end the strike and retract our demands. If we persisted [they said] they would use force and gas against us.

"Because we rejected this appeal, the authorities turned off the drinking water and stopped all food supplies at 12 noon on 19 May. Then at 9.00 am on 22 May, after we had been on strike and endured hunger and thirst for three days, we were suddenly attacked by large units equipped with truncheons. The camp army and guards were joined by 200 special riot police sent from Tirane.

"After clashes lasting an hour, we were too exhausted by hunger and thirst to carry on the fight. We were finally overwhelmed and handcuffed in pairs. On the prisoners' side no one was killed; the riot police suffered two casualties. We were immediately subjected to the most brutal tortures which went on for 24 hours.

"Then a special military tribunal sent from Tirane sentenced to death four prisoners aged from 24 to 32. They were Skender Demiri, from an orphanage in Tirane; Zef

Pali, from Sukthi in Durres district; Hajri Pashai, from
Llakatund in Vlore district, and Skender Shohollari, from
Pogradec district. Our friends were executed near the camp
at 3.40 pm on 24 May 1973. We all heard the shots.
Besides this, 56 prisoners were given additional sentences
ranging from 10 to 25 years."

The same source stated that he had been informed that a similar
strike took place in 1978, after which three political prisoners
were executed: Vangjel Lezha and Fadil Kokomani, both
previously correspondents for Albania's leading daily *Zeri i
Popullit*, and Xhelal Koprencka, from Korce, who had worked as
a surveyor in Shkoder before his arrest and imprisonment. On this
occasion, too, many other prisoners were reportedly punished with
additional sentences of up to 25 years' imprisonment. (A second
source has independently informed Amnesty International of the
execution of Xhelal Koprencka in 1978 after a strike by
prisoners.)

Ballsh labour camp 309/1

Ballsh labour camp, near the town of Ballsh, in Fier district, is
divided into three sections—for political prisoners (309/1),
ordinary criminals, and foreigners (309/3). When political prisoners
were first brought to Ballsh in the early 1970s they were
employed in the construction of the nearby oil-refinery, which was
being built with Chinese aid. Prisoners were divided into brigades
according to their skills; for instance, a builders' brigade, a brigade
which dug trenches for pipe-laying, a carpenters' brigade, a
brigade which made moulds for concrete.

At present Ballsh 309/1 is primarily a camp for the elderly and
those unfit for work. Most political prisoners there do not work,
except for a small number employed on farmland attached to the
camp. In other respects, however, conditions there are described
as similar to those in Spac, but less harsh. The daily schedule for
prisoners who worked on the construction of the oil-refinery was
reportedly as follows: they were woken at 4.30 am, had breakfast
and roll-call at 5.00 am and began to work at 6.00 am. At
3.00 pm they returned to the camp. The main meal was at
3.30 pm, after which prisoners might wash and mend their clothes
or cook, until 6.00 pm, when they were given tea. Lights out was
at 10.00 pm.

Prisoners are housed in prefabricated barracks and appear to
suffer from the cold more than at Spac; this may perhaps be
because many of them are elderly. In winter most prisoners sleep
fully-clothed. The barracks are equipped with loudspeakers

which transmit radio broadcasts between 6.00 pm and 10.00 pm. In 1979 the camp acquired a television set.

The two main meals in the early 1980s were said to consist of soup containing 120g of vegetables (leeks and cabbage) and 7g of oil, divided between the meals at 5.00 am and 3.30 pm. At the latter meal the soup contained also beans, rice or macaroni and 35g of meat (75g of meat for working prisoners). The daily ration included 800g of bread and, in the evening, tea with 10g of sugar. Prisoners whose families sent them money (after work ceased at Ballsh they no longer received wages) could buy vegetables (tomatoes, peppers and potatoes) produced on the camp farm, and macaroni, rice and oil in limited quantities from the camp shop.

Ballsh 309/3

In 1972, when Albanian political prisoners were first brought to Ballsh, a number of prisoners of foreign origin were transferred to a separate section of Ballsh, 309/3. They reportedly consisted of some 14 Greeks and 20 Yugoslavs, who until then had been in Burrel prison. In 1981 there were between 25 and 30 foreign prisoners in 309/3, almost all of them Yugoslavs or Greeks (the latter including refugees who had settled in Albania after the Greek civil war of the late 1940s). Some prisoners in Ballsh 309/3 were reportedly serving sentences of between seven and 10 years' imprisonment after conviction on charges of "anti-state agitation and propaganda"; others, who had been convicted of espionage or sabotage, were serving sentences of between 15 and 25 years' imprisonment.

The inmates of 309/3 sleep in one large room and in summer spend the greater part of the day in the prison courtyard (they do not work). The regime for foreigners appears to be somewhat better than for Albanian political prisoners—for instance, they reportedly receive a daily meat ration of 75g (as opposed to 35g for Albanians). Joseph Valyrakis, a Greek, who was detained in Ballsh 309/3 from late 1972 to the end of 1973, described prison life as follows:

"We were woken up at 5.00 am by the sound of blows on a hanging metal pipe; at the same time, the radio was connected to loudspeakers. We had breakfast and then went out into the courtyard (20m by 10m) and lined up for roll-call. In winter the courtyard was covered with mud. After the roll-call the greatest problem was how to pass the time until the midday meal. At about 10.00 am the first quarrels of the day always started: about food, bread, the cook, or disputes about card games and that sort of thing—or for no apparent reason. Sometimes, these quarrels got out of hand and many people became involved; some would be injured or sent into solitary confinement. At 12 noon, there was the midday meal and at 2.00 pm a further roll-call in the courtyard. At 3.00 pm we heard the news over the loud-speaker. 5.00 pm was the most critical time of the day: bread was distributed. There were frequent rows—the cook would discover that some rations had been stolen. Then came dinner and at 6.00 pm we went out into the courtyard again for the last roll-call of the day. From 7.00 pm on there was silence. We had to undress and go to bed. No one was allowed to walk about, except in his underwear."

The conditions in 309/3 had, according to one report, somewhat improved by 1980.

Burrel prison (Mat district)

Burrel prison is Albania's most ill-famed prison—many of the political prisoners detained from the late 1940s to the 1960s died there. A number of disgraced and convicted former Party officials are said to be held there now, along with other political prisoners, many of whom are serving long sentences.

Joseph Valyrakis, who was held in Burrel for several months in late 1972, stated that the cells were unheated and that in winter snow blew in through their broken windows. An Albanian political prisoner who was in Burrel from 1968 to 1972 alleged that he was held in a damp basement cell with 32 other prisoners. When he first arrived at Burrel prisoners slept on the bare cement floor, he said, although they were eventually given boards.

Conditions are still extremely harsh and primitive, according to several prisoners held there as late as 1982, and it is alleged that it is common for political prisoners to be beaten and punished with solitary confinement.

Tirane prison 313

This prison is reportedly situated on the road leading from the centre of town to the Tirane cinema studios. The prison is part of a complex of buildings occupied by the ordinary police and the *Sigurimi*. On the opposite side of the road are civilian, military and prison hospitals. Prisoners are held for investigation in one section of Tirane prison separate from another holding prisoners serving sentences or being detained pending transfer. Amnesty

International has little information about conditions in Tirane prison.

Internment

Internment may be imposed by a court as a supplementary penalty—for example, one former political prisoner has reported that he was sentenced in the late 1970s to three years' imprisonment followed by three years' internment at a camp on the Cape of Rodon. In other cases former political prisoners have, on release, been administratively interned in various parts of the country.

Probably the largest number of people affected by administratively imposed internment are members of families who have incurred the disapproval of the authorities, often because their relatives have fled abroad. In many cases such families have been deported to areas far from their homes, in order to carry out land reclamation work (particularly on the coastal marshes).

One example reported to Amnesty International concerns a Muslim family from Korce district. In the late 1960s, after a number of relatives had fled the country, they were interned on a state farm in Shtyllas, Fier district, and worked on a drainage project for six years together with 25 other families from Korce district, from the villages of Bilisht, Bracanji, Rakicke, Poncare and Vidohove. Work was carried out under the supervision of guards, and the internees lived in wooden barracks housing four to six families each.

A Greek citizen, Vanghelis Kazandzis, who crossed the border into Albania in 1972 to avoid conscription under the military regime in Greece, was interned in the village of Clirim, close to Fier. Here he worked on the state farm until his arrest on charges of "anti-state agitation and propaganda" in 1979. Other foreigners, most of them Greek refugees who had lived for many years in Albania, were also reportedly interned there. Internees were paid a daily rate of 15 leks for their work on the state farm.

An example in which internment appears to have been indefinitely prolonged concerns the Lekas family, ethnic Greeks from Gline, in Gjirokaster district. In 1951 this family was deported and interned in Gjonas, in Lushnje district. Although at least one of the children was later allowed to return to relatives in Gline in order to attend a Greek-language school, other members of the family were still living in Lushnje district by the beginning of the 1980s and had successively been interned in the villages of Halilaj, Kolonje and Rrapeze.

Case histories

The names of five of the people whose case histories appear below are being kept confidential either at their own or their relatives' request.

A. A manual worker, born in southern Albania in 1928 and of Orthodox Christian origin, he served a total of over 29 years' imprisonment between 1950 and the beginning of the 1980s.

He was first arrested in 1950 on charges of anti-state activity, being accused of having written anti-government slogans on walls and of having distributed leaflets criticizing the authorities. He was allegedly the victim of an *agent provocateur*. At a closed trial he was sentenced to 18 years' imprisonment; the sentence was confirmed on appeal. He served it in a series of labour camps where he worked on the construction of a meat processing factory (Tirane); a military airport (near Berat); marsh drainage (Skrofotine, near Vlore); irrigation (Shtyllas) and dam construction (Hajmel on the River Drin near Shkoder).

He was released early, at the beginning of the 1960s. Unable to find employment, he tried to flee the country shortly afterwards, but was arrested, and sentenced to 25 years' imprisonment by a military court for "attempted flight from the state". He served his second sentence in labour camps, building blocks of flats in Tirane, cement factories in Elbasan and Fush-Kruje, a caustic soda factory in Vlore and an oil-refinery in Ballsh. He was released at the beginning of the 1980s after having obtained a reduction of sentence in 1962 as a result of an amnesty and a further subsequent reduction in return for exceeding work norms.

B. A craftsman of Muslim origin, born in 1940 in central Albania, he served some 17 years' imprisonment before his release in 1980.

In 1963, dissatisfied with economic conditions and following conflict with local authorities, he had tried to flee the country. He was arrested near the border and subsequently sentenced by a military court to 18 years' imprisonment and three years' loss of voting rights.

He served his sentence as follows: from 1964 to 1968 in labour camps in Vlore, Elbasan and Fush-Kruje; 1968 to 1972, Burrel prison; 1972 to 1975, Ballsh labour camp; at the end of 1975 he was moved to Spac labour camp. He was conditionally released in 1980, about a year before his sentence was due to expire.

C. A technician, born in 1938 in central Albania and of Orthodox Christian origin, he was imprisoned for more than 11 years. He was arrested in 1966 while trying to flee the country and sentenced in 1967 to 12 years' imprisonment. He served his sentence in labour camps in Lac, Vlore (Skrofotine) and, from 1969, in Spac, where he remained until his release in 1978, several months before the expiry date of his sentence.

D. This former prisoner, of Muslim origin, was born in 1958 in northern Albania. He was arrested in 1980 while doing military service and tried in 1981 on charges of "anti-state agitation and propaganda". The charges reportedly claimed that he had expressed criticism of the ruling Albanian Party of Labour and had spoken favourably of King Zog, Albania's pre-war ruler, in the presence of other conscripts. At his trial, which was open, he pleaded not guilty. He was not granted the services of a legal adviser. The court found him guilty and sentenced him to eight years' imprisonment. He was sent to serve his sentence in Spac labour camp and was almost certainly released under the amnesty of November 1982.

E. A skilled worker, born in 1939 and of Muslim origin, he was sentenced in 1979 to three years' imprisonment and three years' internment.

Arrested in 1979 he was held for investigation on charges of "anti-state agitation and propaganda". He was accused of having criticized the Albanian political system in conversations with friends and of having referred to strikes by prisoners in Spac. He denied the charges against him. He refused to sign a confession and is reported to have been beaten with a rubber truncheon during interrogation. At his trial he was accused of being an opponent of the government and of having a politically undesirable past. The trial was open but he was not granted a legal adviser. He was sent to serve his sentence of imprisonment in Spac labour camp and was afterwards interned on the Cape of Rodon.

Theodosios Lekas

He is in Spac labour camp serving a sentence of 25 years' imprisonment imposed in 1978.

Born in 1920 in the village of Gline, Gjirokaster district, he is an ethnic Greek. In 1951 he and his wife and children were deported to Gjonas, in Lushnje district in central Albania, after he had apparently expressed pro-Greek sentiments. In the following years the family was successively interned in the villages of Halilaj, Kolonje and Rrapeze, in Lushnje.

The following account comes from his two sons, who fled to Greece in 1982:

He was arrested in January 1978 after police had searched his house in Kolonje and confiscated a religious book and family photographs. He was detained in Lushnje for investigation on charges of "anti-state agitation and propaganda". On 30 May 1978 he was tried by the district court of Lushnje; the trial was open. He was then said to have been in poor health and to have suffered a severe loss in weight. He was reportedly accused of having commented on Albania's rift with China and of having stated that Greece and Yugoslavia could profit territorially from Albania's difficulties. In addition, he appears to have been charged with assisting Greek armed forces during the Second World War by showing them routes in the area. The court sentenced him to 25 years' imprisonment and he was sent to Spac labour camp.

Ilias Fanis

Born in 1957 in Finiq, Sarande district, he is an ethnic Greek who was arrested on 11 May 1977 in Finiq at a public meeting at which he was denounced as an enemy of the people. The following is his account of succeeding events:

He was taken by car to Sarande police station and on the way there was beaten by police. He was detained for investigation but was not ill-treated to begin with. However, after he had refused to collaborate with the police he was punched in the face and on one occasion threatened with electric shock torture. At first he shared a cell with a prisoner whom he suspected of being an *agent provocateur*. He was later held in solitary confinement and was not allowed to be visited by relatives, or to receive food from them.

At his trial by the district court of Sarande in August 1977 he was charged with "anti-state agitation and propaganda". The charges reportedly included allegations that he had spoken insultingly of Albania's leader, Enver Hoxha, and that he had

50

made mocking comments about the Albanian army. The trial began in open court, but after Ilias Fanis had threatened to refer to his ill-treatment during investigation, the public was excluded, with the exception of the accused's parents. The court found him guilty and sentenced him to eight years' imprisonment. He refused to appeal against his sentence.

Immediately after his conviction he was brought back to Sarande police station. Some days later he was transferred to Tirane central prison and shortly afterwards to Spac labour camp. He was released early, in November 1982, under the amnesty that year.

Vanghelis Kazandzis

A former medical student, born in Athens in 1949, he was sentenced in 1979 to nine years' imprisonment but was pardoned and allowed to return to Greece in 1981. His account of events is as follows:

He crossed the border into Albania in October 1972 in order to avoid conscription under the the military regime in Greece. He presented himself to the Albanian border guards and was taken to Sarande police station, where he was interrogated and held for over a month but was not ill-treated. In November 1972 he was sent to work in the state agricultural enterprise in the village of Clirim, near Fier.

He was arrested on 19 July 1979, apparently because the authorities suspected that he wished to return to Greece. They charged him with "anti-state agitation and propaganda" and he was held in Fier police station for 13 months, pending trial. He shared a ground floor cell with several other prisoners. It was clean but damp. Detainees slept on boards and had blankets but no mattress. They were given very little food. Although he was not systematically ill-treated, he was beaten on a number of occasions during interrogations and the screws on his handcuffs were tightened in order to cause pain. In this way he was induced to sign a "confession".

On 18 August 1980 he was tried by the district court of Fier. The trial was open, but he was not granted a legal adviser. He was charged with having criticized the Albanian political system and with having watched a Yugoslav television program — in fact, a televised football game—containing anti-Albanian progaganda. Several villagers from Clirim gave evidence against him. They are said to have contradicted themselves and one of the witnesses was allegedly drunk at the time. When Vanghelis Kazandzis protested that he had not been shown the full materials of his case, as was his right by law, the procurator reprimanded him and accused him of trying to slander socialist justice. He was found guilty and sentenced to nine years' imprisonment.

After the trial he was returned to Fier for a month, then transferred to Tirane prison, where he was detained in a room together with some 60 other political prisoners. At the end of November 1980 he was sent to Ballsh camp's section for foreigners (309/3), where he shared a barracks with some 30 other prisoners. In October 1981 he was pardoned and allowed to return to Greece.

Ram Sejda

Originally a Yugoslav citizen (he was born in Kosovo in 1927), he was administratively interned for more than 11 years and later tried and imprisoned for five years.

Ram Sejda emigrated legally to Albania in 1964 to join relatives there. He was initially employed in construction work, and then either in 1965 or early 1966 he, his mother and brother were interned in the village of Bilce, close to Berat; here he worked as an agricultural labourer.

The three eventually applied to the authorities for permission to return to Yugoslavia, but for a number of years received no satisfactory response.

In December 1977 they went to Tirane without first getting official permission to leave their place of internment—they went to the capital in the hope of pressing their request to return to Yugoslavia. While they were at the Ministry of the Interior in Tirane, police arrested Ram Sejda and his brother and took them back to Berat.

Ram Sejda, who was held in solitary confinement in Berat during investigation proceedings, was taken to hospital and forcibly fed after he had engaged in a hunger-strike which lasted 45 days. He was apparently repeatedly asked by investigators to confess that he had criticized Albania and its leader, Enver Hoxha, and that he had spread propaganda in favour of Yugoslavia and listened to that country's *Radio Pristina*. He was also accused of having been in contact with people who had conspired against the state. He denied all these charges. He later alleged that he had been beaten during interrogation, and that the screws of his handcuffs were deliberately tightened in order to inflict pain.

At his trial in 1978 he was charged with "anti-state agitation and propaganda". Three witnesses gave evidence against him— one was a political prisoner of Yugoslav origin who was serving a 20-year sentence in Ballsh labour camp. Ram Sejda was found guilty and sentenced to five years' imprisonment. (His brother reportedly received a 10-month prison sentence for travelling to Tirane without official permission.) After conviction, Ram Sejda was detained in Berat and then, in June 1978, sent to Ballsh labour camp 309/3 for foreigners. He was released under the amnesty of November 1982, three weeks before the expiry date of his sentence. In March 1983 he was allowed to return to Yugoslavia.

Amnesty International —
a worldwide campaign

In recent years, people throughout the world have become more and more aware of the urgent need to protect human rights effectively in every part of the world.

● Countless men and women are in prison for their beliefs. They are being held as prisoners of conscience in scores of countries—in crowded jails, in labour camps and in remote prisons.

● Thousands of political prisoners are being held under administrative detention orders and denied any possibility of a trial or an appeal.

● Others are forcibly confined in psychiatric hospitals or secret detention camps.

● Many are forced to endure relentless, systematic torture.

● More than a hundred countries retain the death penalty.

● Political leaders and ordinary citizens are becoming the victims of abductions, "disappearances" and killings, carried out both by government forces and opposition groups.

An international effort

To end secret arrests, torture and killing requires organized and worldwide effort. Amnesty International is part of that effort.

Launched as an independent organization over 20 years ago, Amnesty International is open to anyone prepared to work universally for the release of prisoners of conscience, for fair trials for political prisoners and for an end to torture and executions.

The movement now has members and supporters in more than 160 countries. It is independent of any government, political group, ideology, economic interest or religious creed.

It began with a newspaper article, "The Forgotten Prisoners", published on 28 May 1961 in *The Observer* (London) and reported in *Le Monde* (Paris).

Announcing an impartial campaign to help victims of political persecution, the British lawyer Peter Benenson wrote:

Open your newspaper any day of the week and you will find a report from somewhere in the world of someone being imprisoned, tortured or executed because his opinions or religion are unacceptable to his government. . . . The newspaper reader feels a sickening sense of impotence. Yet if these feelings of disgust all over the world could be united into common action, something effective could be done.

Within a week he had received more than a thousand offers of support—to collect information, publicize it and approach governments. The groundwork was laid for a permanent human rights organization that eventually became known as Amnesty International. The first chairperson of its International Executive Committee (from 1963 to 1974) was Sean MacBride, who received the Nobel Peace Prize in 1974 and the Lenin Prize in 1975.

The mandate

Amnesty International is playing a specific role in the international protection of human rights.

It seeks the *release* of men and women detained anywhere because of their beliefs, colour, sex, ethnic origin, language or religious creed, provided they have not used or advocated violence. These are termed *prisoners of conscience*.

It works for *fair and prompt trials* for *all political prisoners* and works on behalf of such people detained without charge or trial.

It opposes the *death penalty* and *torture* or other cruel, inhuman or degrading treatment or punishment of *all prisoners* without reservation.

Amnesty International acts on the basis of the Universal Declaration of Human Rights and other international convenants. Amnesty International is convinced of the indivisibility and mutual dependence of all human rights. Through the practical work for prisoners within its mandate, Amnesty International participates in the wider promotion and protection of human rights in the civil, political, economic, social and cultural spheres.

Amnesty International does not oppose or support any government or political system. Its members around the world include supporters of differing systems who agree on the defence of all people in all countries against imprisonment for their beliefs, and against torture and execution.

Amnesty International at work

The working methods of Amnesty International are based on the principle of international responsibility for the protection of human rights. The movement tries to take action wherever and whenever there are violations of those human rights falling within its mandate. Since it was founded, Amnesty International groups have intervened on behalf of more than 25,000 prisoners in over a hundred countries with widely differing ideologies.

A unique aspect of the work of Amnesty International groups— placing the emphasis on the need for *international* human rights work—is the fact that each group works on behalf of prisoners held in countries other than its own. At least two prisoner cases are assigned to each group; the cases are balanced geographically and politically to ensure impartiality.

There are now 3,341 local Amnesty International groups throughout the world. There are sections in 43 countries (in Africa, Asia, the Americas, Europe and the Middle East) and individual members, subscribers and supporters in more than 120 other countries. Members do not work on cases in their own countries. No section, group or member is expected to provide information on their own country and no section, group or member has any responsibility for action taken or statements issued by the international organization concerning their own country.

Continuous research

The movement attaches the highest importance to balanced and accurate reporting of facts. All its activities depend on meticulous research into allegations of human rights violations. The International Secretariat in London (with a staff of 175, comprising 30 nationalities) has a Research Department which collects and analyses information from a wide variety of sources. These include hundreds of newspapers and journals, government bulletins, transcriptions of radio broadcasts, reports from lawyers and humanitarian organizations, as well as letters from prisoners and their families. Amnesty International also sends fact-finding missions for on-the-spot investigations and to observe trials, meet prisoners and interview government officials. Amnesty International takes full responsibility for its published reports and if proved wrong on any point is prepared to issue a correction.

Once the relevant facts are established, information is sent to sections and groups for action. The members then start the work of trying to protect the individuals whose human rights are reported to have been violated. They send letters to government ministers and embassies. They organize public meetings, arrange special publicity events, such as vigils at appropriate government offices or embassies, and try to interest newspapers in the cases they have taken up. They ask their friends and colleagues to help in the effort. They collect signatures for international petitions and raise money to send relief, such as medicine, food and clothing, to the prisoners and their families.

A permanent campaign

In addition to case work on behalf of individual prisoners, Amnesty International members campaign for the abolition of torture and the death penalty. This includes trying to prevent torture and executions when people have been taken to known torture centres or sentenced to death. Volunteers in dozens of countries can be alerted in such cases, and within hours hundreds of telegrams and other appeals can be on their way to the government, prison or detention centre.

Symbol of
Amnesty International

Amnesty International condemns as a matter of principle the torture and execution of prisoners by *anyone*, including opposition groups. Governments have the responsibility of dealing with such abuses, acting in conformity with international standards for the protection of human rights.

In its efforts to mobilize world public opinion, Amnesty International neither supports nor opposes economic or cultural boycotts. It *does* take a stand against the international transfer of military, police or security equipment and expertise likely to be used by recipient governments to detain prisoners of conscience and to inflict torture and carry out executions.

Amnesty International does not grade governments or countries according to their record on human rights. Not only does repression in various countries prevent the free flow of information about human rights abuses, but the techniques of repression and their impact vary widely. Instead of attempting comparisons, Amnesty International concentrates on trying to end the specific violations of human rights in each case.

Policy and funds

Amnesty International is a democratically run movement. Every two years major policy decisions are taken by an International Council comprising representatives from all the sections. They elect an International Executive Committee to carry out their decisions and supervise the day-to-day running of the International Secretariat.

The organization is financed by its members throughout the world, by individual subscriptions and donations. Members pay fees and conduct fund-raising campaigns—they organize concerts and art auctions and are often to be seen on fund-raising drives at street corners in their neighbourhoods.

Its rules about accepting donations are strict and ensure that any funds received by any part of the organization do not compromise it in any way, affect its integrity, make it dependent on any donor, or limit its freedom of activity.

The organization's accounts are audited annually and are published with its annual report.

Amnesty International has formal relations with the United Nations (ECOSOC), UNESCO, the Council of Europe, the Organization of African Unity and the Organization of American States.

How to subscribe to Amnesty International

A subscription to Amnesty International will give you access to new—often unpublished—information about human rights abuses on a global, independent and impartial basis. By subscribing to Amnesty International you will also receive details about how you can help the people who are the victims.

Amnesty International Newsletter

This monthly bulletin is a regular update on Amnesty International's work: reports of fact-finding missions, details about political prisoners, reliable reports of torture and executions. It is written—without political bias—for human rights activists throughout the world and is widely used by journalists, students, political leaders, medical doctors, lawyers and other professionals.

Amnesty International Report

This annual report is a country-by-country survey of Amnesty International's work to combat political imprisonment, torture and the death penalty throughout the world. The report is organized into sections and normally covers at least 100 countries. It is probably the most widely read—and most influential—of the many reports published by Amnesty International each year.

Annual newsletter subscription: £ 5.00 (US$12.50)
Subscription to both the newsletter and report:
£10.00 (US$25.00)

Amnesty International Publications Catalogue

The Amnesty International publications catalogue lists all recent major Amnesty International reports and documents, together with a selection of earlier publications still in print. It is available, free of charge, from Amnesty International Publications.

Write to: **Amnesty International Publications, 1 Easton Street, London WC1X 8DJ, United Kingdom,** or your local section.